GO FISH

STUDY GUIDE

GO
FISH

STUDY GUIDE

ANDY STANLEY

Multnomah Books

GO FISH STUDY GUIDE

© 2005 by North Point Ministries, Inc.
International Standard Book Number: 978-1-59052-548-7

Cover design by Andrew Cochran at Circle@Seven Studio
Cover photo by Brandon Ching

Unless otherwise indicated, Scripture quotations are from:
The Holy Bible, New International Version
© 1973, 1984 by International Bible Society,
used by permission of Zondervan Publishing House

Published in the United States by Multnomah, an imprint of the Crown
Publishing Group, a division of Penguin Random House LLC, New York.

MULTNOMAH® and its mountain colophon are registered trademarks
of Penguin Random House LLC.

Printed in the United States of America

17 — 13

Contents

Invest and Invite

E very fisherman has a favorite technique. And at North Point Ministries, ours is a strategy we call "Invest and Invite." It's a two-step process of investing in the lives of our unchurched friends, then simply inviting them to church.

INVEST

We invest in other people when we spend our time and energy building relationships with them. You can be strategic about these friendships wherever God has placed you—at work, in the neighborhood, or in community activities. Friendships pave the way for influence, enabling you to impact lives for Christ.

INVITE

Many people think evangelism involves giving a polished, compelling spiritual presentation. But it doesn't have to be that way. North Point

Community Church is designed to be an environment where unchurched people can feel comfortable while they investigate matters of faith. So when the time is right, invite them to church. Then make yourself available to answer the questions that will arise.

So, as you immerse yourself in the concepts in *Go Fish,* keep in mind the role that your local church is intended to play as your fishing partner.

Fishy Motives

by Andy Stanley

What was it that motivated you to become a Christian? When you think back, what was foremost in your mind when you made the decision to follow Christ? Was it your need for salvation? Were you seeking a sense of peace? Perhaps you were motivated by the idea that God could help you get your life in order. Whatever your motivation, you probably didn't become a Christian so you could tell other people about Jesus, did you? In fact, becoming a salesman for Christianity was just about the last thing on your mind.

And yet, of all the changes Jesus promised His followers, making them "fishers of men" was at the top of the list. Regardless of your initial motives for receiving Christ, that's what He wants for you as well.

When we examine the Gospels, one thing is clear about Jesus' disciples: Followers become fishers. It's what Jesus predicted when He called the first believers. And it's exactly what happened to them as the rest of the New Testament unfolded.

The problem for most of us is that telling people about Jesus doesn't exactly come naturally. In fact, it can be awkward, unappreciated, and uncomfortable. But as we'll discover in the coming weeks together, it's not really optional. Because God's design is to use the people He's reached to reach other people. And that can only happen if we answer the call to go fish.

We Were All Fish Once

When Jesus called His first followers, He had very clear intentions: "I will make you fishers of men." He didn't mention refining their characters, making them better people, or even saving them from their sins—although He did those things too. But of all the things He could have emphasized, Jesus announced that His primary agenda for those who follow Him is to use them to introduce others to their loving heavenly Father. It was true in Jesus' time. And it's still true today.

But that can be intimidating... How do you do it? What do you say? And what if they don't want to hear it? In this session, we'll reveal an important perspective that cuts through all the obstacles that keep Christians from fishing for men. From this refreshing point of view, you will experience a natural motivation to get in on this part of God's agenda for the world. And along the way, we'll see how God has placed each of us in the perfect place to follow Him and become fishers of men.

PRAY *WHAT*?!

God's desire is to take our lives on this earth and leverage them for eternal value by using us to introduce His children to everlasting life. Nevertheless, most of our prayers center around the things of this temporary world. In the space below, list some of the subjects that are most predominant in your prayer life.

Based on the subjects you listed, approximately what percentage of your prayer time is devoted to eternal things like fishing for men?

VIDEO NOTES

From the video message, fill in the blanks:

1. Most people become Christians for purely
   _____ motives.
2. The first disciples followed Jesus because of
   what He did for _____ .
3. God wants to lead us to become fishers of
   _____ .

> " The Christian life is a process
> of laying down our agendas
> and getting in on God's. "

NOTES

DISCUSSION QUESTIONS

Take a few moments to discuss your answers to these questions with the group.

1. What are the agendas of most people who become Christians?
2. Why do you think the disciples first wanted to follow Jesus?
3. According to Jesus, what is His agenda for His followers?
4. What obstacles keep you from being a fisher of men?
5. Talk about the person who was key in you becoming a Christian.
6. Who is someone that God has perfectly positioned you to influence?

MILEPOSTS

- Often, people's initial motives for following Christ are selfish ones.

- Jesus promised to make His followers into fishers of men.

- Every follower is a prime candidate to fish for men.

WHAT WILL YOU DO?

This week, write a brief thank-you letter to the person or people who took the time to make sure you understood the gospel message of salvation and the invitation to enter into a relationship with God through Christ. You do not have to send the letter in order to complete this assignment.

THINK ABOUT IT

Thinking about the person who introduced you to Christ, what unique platform did that person occupy in your life that enabled him or her to be heard by you?

What unique platform(s) do you occupy that God might want to use to make Himself known to the non-believers in your world?

CHANGING YOUR MIND

As you meditate on God's Word, it becomes easier to envision His agenda of making us fishers of men.

"'Come, follow me,' Jesus said,
'and I will make you fishers of men.'"

MARK 1:17

LAST WEEK...

In the last session we saw that Jesus had one clear goal in mind for His followers. It wasn't just to make them more holy or more disciplined or more loving. He promised to make them "fishers of men." And as we saw, He has the same agenda for us today when we decide to follow Him.

Why Fish?

I n our culture, the idea of a Christian sharing his faith with a non-Christian makes a lot of people uncomfortable. Many non-Christians dread the thought of being assaulted and proselytized by zealous "born agains." And many Christians fear being rejected, ridiculed, or humiliated for trying to push their beliefs on someone else. Both parties find it much easier just to keep to themselves on matters of faith and avoid conflict altogether. But the Bible is clear that followers are to become fishers. And fishing means being strategic with our opportunities to tell others about Jesus.

In this session, we'll look at one of the most compelling—and overlooked—reasons why Christians should be active about sharing their faith. And in the process we'll examine why telling others about Jesus doesn't mean you have to be pushy or overbearing. Nor does it mean you have to embarrass yourself in front of friends and co-workers. In fact, fishing can become a natural part of your personality. And once you understand the reasons why you need to fish, it can be one of the most motivating discoveries you've had since you first became a Christian.

EXERCISE

TURNING POINTS

History is measured by landmark events that shape the course of mankind. In the space below, write down five events that changed the world during the 1900s.

> " A belief system is always
> subject to argument.
> But historical facts are
> irrefutable. "

VIDEO NOTES

From the video message, fill in the blanks:

1. Christians believe something _____ in history.

2. We think talking about Jesus gets us into a _____ about belief systems.

3. Being a fisher of men isn't about having so much _____ that you can refute the skeptics.

NOTES

DISCUSSION QUESTIONS

Take a few moments to discuss your answers to these questions with the group.

1. Have you ever seen something so exciting that you couldn't stop talking about it? Describe.
2. What's the difference between sharing something you believe and sharing something you've seen and heard?
3. Does being a fisher of men mean convincing someone of your beliefs? Why or why not?
4. Have you ever been asked a tough question about your faith? How did you respond?
5. How would your life be different if you had never heard anything about Jesus?

MILEPOSTS

- The first apostles couldn't stop talking about what they had seen and heard.

- Christianity did not begin as a new belief system. It began as an event in history.

- Christians need to talk about Jesus because the message is so counterintuitive—if nobody tells them, they won't know.

WHAT WILL YOU DO?

This week, your homework is to consider the major events in your personal history that have occured as a result of Christ's interaction in your life. What are some of the undeniable facts about you that can only be attributed to the work of Christ?

THINK ABOUT IT

Can you imagine sharing your faith in terms of the significant events that have happened to you personally as a result of knowing Christ as your personal savior? In the space below, describe how you would convey your story to another person in the form of an account of the events that you have "seen and heard."

CHANGING YOUR MIND

Before Jesus returned to heaven He left His followers with marching orders. Meditate this week on the Great Commission and how you can share with others what you have seen and heard.

"Therefore go and make disciples of all nations, baptizing them in the name of the Father and of the Son and of the Holy Spirit."

MATTHEW 28:19

LAST WEEK...

In the last session we saw that Christianity began as an event in history, not as a new belief system. Likewise, sharing your faith is not so much about convincing someone to believe something as it is telling them about what you have seen and heard.

Fish Guts

Telling others about Jesus can be intimidating, overwhelming, and even disturbing. There's something about trying to convince another person to adopt a whole new belief system that seems daunting and uncomfortable. "Who am I to say what another person should believe?" we wonder.

But if you think talking about Jesus is difficult for us today, consider how intimidating it must have been for the first believers. We stand to experience a little awkwardness, but they faced total rejection from society, persecution, or even death. And yet somehow they persisted. Because they did, we're still talking about Jesus' death and resurrection more than two thousand years later. So why did they do it? What could possibly have given them the courage to speak when they did?

In this session, we'll examine the driving force behind the boldness of the first believers. And we'll see how the same factors that fostered courage in the first century are still in place today, giving our generation the guts to fish.

THE DADDY DIFFERENCE

Name a situation that a child is afraid to face alone, but is willing to face if her daddy is with her. Have you ever experienced such a situation?

Why does the presence of a parent change the child's perception of this situation?

EXERCISE

> " *All fear dissipates like vapor when God is deemed sovereign over that which is feared.* "

VIDEO NOTES

From the video message, fill in the blanks:

1. In light of God's sovereignty over the events in their lives, the believers in Acts 4 prayed for _____ .

2. Boldness is simply _____ up when the opportunity pops up.

NOTES

DISCUSSION QUESTIONS

Take a few moments to discuss your answers to these questions with the group.

1. Why do you think the disciples in Acts 4:31 were filled with boldness?

2. How would your life be different if you truly believed God was in control?

3. What are the threats that deter you from speaking God's Word boldly?

4. How might God use those threats for His own glory?

5. How do your prayers differ from the one prayed in Acts 4?

6. Have you ever asked God to enable you to speak with boldness? Why or why not?

7. What would "bold" look like in your life?

MILEPOSTS

- God, who is sovereign, has invited us to be players in the most important activity in the universe.

- Boldness is simply speaking up when the opportunity pops up.

WHAT WILL YOU DO?

This week, commit to pray daily for boldness to share the story of God's work in your life when the opportunities present themselves. Be prepared to discuss your experiences with the group.

THINK ABOUT IT

Think about the person you listed in session one, the person who you have been perfectly positioned by God to influence. What would be a bold move for you this week in his or her life? (We're not talking about a megaphone and a sandwich board!) Is there a CD or a book you could give, an invitation to attend church you could extend, or a question you could ask that might lead to a spiritual conversation?

CHANGING YOUR MIND

When you think about the good news that we have to share, it seems silly to think that we would be afraid. Meditate this week on the amazing grace that is offered to us through Jesus.

"For God did not send his Son into the world to condemn the world, but to save the world through him."

JOHN 3:17

LAST WEEK...

Last week, we explored important truths about our role in God's plan for the world. In essence, we are in the middle of the fulfillment of His promise to present the gospel of Jesus to all mankind. That realization gave the first believers tremendous courage to share their faith, and it can be a great source of boldness for us as well.

Fishing Buddies

So far, we've talked about the reasons to fish, the courage to fish, and the fact that we are living during the "fishing season" of God's plan for the world. But no matter how much you understand the need to fish, and no matter how motivated you are to do it, there's still something intimidating about getting up the courage to tell someone about Jesus. We picture ourselves alone with a lost friend, awkwardly turning the conversation to the subject of spirituality. Or we dread facing a theological question we can't answer. And deep inside, we know that making them uncomfortable might make them resist God even more. After all, that's part of what they don't like about Christianity in the first place.

But maybe we have it all wrong. Somewhere in the past, perhaps we locked in on some assumptions about fishing that simply aren't true. Maybe God had something else in mind all along. In this session, we'll examine the amazing power of using the buddy system when it comes to fishing.

COME AND SEE

EXERCISE

Taking turns around the group, have each person "introduce" a famous personality by describing him or her. At first, do not reveal unique accomplishments or characteristics of the person that would give away his or her identity. Add clues until someone guesses the character's identity.

Which is harder: to introduce someone by telling about him, or to let everyone see the person for themselves? Why?

> " The next best thing to meeting Jesus in person is to experience the body of Christ when it functions like it's supposed to. "

VIDEO NOTES

From the video message, fill in the blanks:

1. Being in a community of believers breaks down the barriers to _____ .
2. When the church is organized and strategized around official _____ business, Jesus shows up in its midst.
3. The _____ is the most powerful, persuasive environment on the planet.

NOTES

DISCUSSION QUESTIONS

Take a few moments to discuss your answers to these questions with the group.

1. Do you tend to think of evangelism as a solo expedition or a partnership? Why?

2. What are some of the biggest differences between evangelizing alone and partnering with other believers to fish for men?

3. Would you be comfortable inviting a non-believer to your church? Why or why not?

4. Describe an environment in which you would be comfortable inviting a non-believing friend to hear more about Jesus.

5. How would you follow up with a friend after he attended church (or another environment) with you?

6. Is there an event in the next month to which you could invite a friend? How would you extend this invitation?

MILEPOSTS

■ Fishing was never meant to be a solo expedition. It's a partnership that involves the body of Christ.

■ Whenever we gather on official Jesus business, God is there in our midst.

■ When unbelievers experience a community of believers, their resistance softens.

WHAT WILL YOU DO?

This week, examine your assumptions about fishing for men. Do you picture it as a solo event in which you need to be prepared to argue theological subjects? Or is it your goal to help cultivate environments in which unbelievers can experience the body of Christ? In the space below, describe your idea of fishing before this session.

THINK ABOUT IT

How can you begin to move toward a model of fishing that involves partnering with other believers? In the space below, describe in detail some ways you can begin to function within the body of Christ to create environments that will give unbelievers the chance to hear about Jesus.

CHANGING YOUR MIND

Fishing is not a solo expedition. This week reflect on how God uses many people to draw us into a growing relationship with Him.

"I planted the seed, Apollos watered it,
but God made it grow."

1 CORINTHIANS 3:6–7

LAST WEEK...

Last week, we saw that the fishing process was never intended to be a solo expedition. Instead, telling others about Jesus is more about exposing them to the functioning body of Christ than it is convincing them of a belief system. And one of the best ways to encourage that exposure is to help create environments where unbelievers can experience a community of believers.

Muddy Water

One of the biggest challenges of sharing Jesus with a non-believer is navigating through the complexities of Christian theology. In fact, maybe you've shied away from fishing because you weren't confident of your ability to explain all the elements of the doctrine of salvation. Even if you understand that man is born into sin and why bad things happen to good people and how God predestined certain events…that doesn't mean you can explain it all to somebody who's never heard it.

The fact is, oftentimes, Christians make Christianity way too complicated. There are people in this world who have rejected what they think is Christianity; but in reality, they have merely rejected an over-complicated distortion of Christianity. Meanwhile, they're still waiting to experience an authentic version of the love of Jesus.

In this session, we'll learn a simple, clear definition of what it means to be a Christian. And as you become familiar with it, you will be equipped to fish without risk of muddying the waters.

KEEP IT SIMPLE

EXERCISE

Form a circle with your group. Have someone make up a short phrase and whisper it into the ear of the person beside him. Then have the second person whisper it to the third, and so on. (Continue this process until the phrase has been passed all the way around the circle. Do not say the phrase out loud. Do not repeat the phrase—say it only once per person.) When the last person has heard the phrase, have him say it out loud. Now compare it to the original version of the phrase. Did it change? Why is it so hard to transmit a simple message?

" *Christians have the unfortunate talent of turning the blood of Christ into the mud of Christianity.* "

VIDEO NOTES

From the video message, fill in the blanks:

1. To become a Christian, a person needs to know that:

   God _____ .

   God _____ His son.

2. To become a Christian:

   We need to _____ on the work of Jesus.

   Then we _____ the gift of eternal life.

NOTES

DISCUSSION QUESTIONS

Take a few moments to discuss your answers to these questions with the group.

1. Why do you think Christians make Christianity so complicated?

2. How do you think the average person would describe the requirements for getting into heaven?

3. How would you describe those requirements in light of this session?

4. Name two people in your sphere of influence who don't know that God loves them and forgives them.

5. If you had to guess, what are some of the complications that have prevented them from understanding God's simple message?

MILEPOSTS

- Oftentimes, Christians make Christianity too complicated.

- God loves us and He gave His son for us

- When we believe in Jesus we have eternal life.

WHAT WILL YOU DO?

How well can you explain the gospel to someone else? Is it clear and succinct? Or does it involve concepts that only an experienced Christian can understand? This week, memorize the four words from John 3:16 presented in this session.

THINK ABOUT IT

Using the four words from John 3:16 that were highlighted in this session, describe some of the ways you are aware of God's love for you; what it means to you that He gave His son Jesus for you; how you know that you are trusting in Jesus for eternal life. Could you explain these experiences to a non-believing friend?

CHANGING YOUR MIND

Commit to memory this simple summary of the gospel. You will then be able to use it as a guide when discussing the Christian faith with others.

"For God so loved the world that he gave his one and only Son, that whoever believes in him shall not perish but have eternal life."

JOHN 3:16

LAST WEEK...

Last week, we examined the fact that Christians often make Christianity sound complicated. As a result, we sometimes keep non-believers from hearing and understanding the simple message of Christ. Christianity can be summed up in four words from John 3:16: *loved, gave, believe, have.*

The One That Got Away

E very seasoned fisherman has a story of the one that got away. But what about us? Are there neighbors and coworkers all around us that God longs for us to reach out to? Are there old friends or relatives that He's been preparing to hear the good news of salvation? Could we be overlooking the obvious? And if so, what's obscuring our vision?

In this final session, we'll discover a dangerous tendency that can pull Christians away from their calling to become fishers of men. In our effort to soak up the benefits of a new life in Christ, we can easily forget about those who have yet to hear about Jesus. And in the process, we can live our whole lives and miss out on what God intends for us.

From a rather obscure story in the Old Testament comes a powerful principle that can help us stay on track. Through the example of four unlikely men in ancient Samaria, we come face-to-face with a decision that every believer must make in order to answer the call to go fish.

I FORGOT

There are many reasons we can forget something important.
But one of the most popular explanations we give is, "I was
preoccupied with…." Name a few situations in which we
can become preoccupied and forget something important.

- _____

- _____

- _____

What are the causes and solutions for each of the situations named above?

VIDEO NOTES

From the video message, fill in the blanks:

1. The lepers said to each other, "We're not doing
   _____ ."

2. If we're not careful, our tendency will be to
   forget to go _____ .

> " *With great blessing comes
> great responsibility.* "

NOTES

DISCUSSION QUESTIONS

Take a few moments to discuss your answers to these questions with the group.

1. Why do Christians often forget to "go back" and share the good news with others who need it?

2. What riches do you enjoy that need to be shared with others?

3. What would it look like in your life to "cross the desert" just to tell them?

4. How might it change their lives to discover God's riches?

5. From the perspective of those watching from heaven, what do you think is the "obvious" thing for you to do?

MILEPOSTS

- Our tendency as Christians is to forget to tell those we've left behind about Jesus.

- We have an obligation to share the blessings we have received with others.

WHAT WILL YOU DO?

This week, outline a plan for going back to share with others the good news of what you've found. In the space below, list the names of three people you could begin to pray for and with whom you could share the good news of Jesus.

THINK ABOUT IT

As you pray for the people on the list you created above, what is one strategic next step that you could take that might eventually lead to a conversation about Jesus?

CHANGING YOUR MIND

Spend time this week contemplating how great God's love is for us. Use this as the motivation to tell others about this great love that is also available to them.

Dear friends, since God so loved us,
we also ought to love one another."

1 JOHN 4:11

LEADER'S GUIDE

So, You're the Leader...

Is that intimidating? Perhaps exciting? No doubt you have some mental pictures of what it will look like, what you will say, and how it will go. Before you get too far into the planning process, there are some things you should know about leading a small-group discussion. We've compiled some tried and true techniques here to help you.

BASICS ABOUT LEADING

1. **Don't teach…facilitate**—Perhaps you've been in a Sunday school class or Bible study in which the leader could answer any question and always had something interesting to say. It's easy to think you need to be like that too. Relax. You don't. Leading a small group is quite different. Instead of being the featured act at the party, think of yourself as the host or hostess behind the scenes. Your primary job is to create an environment where people feel

comfortable and to keep the meeting generally on track. Your party is most successful when your guests do most of the talking.

2. **Cultivate discussion**—It's also easy to think that the meeting lives or dies by *your* ideas. In reality, what makes a small-group meeting successful are the ideas of everyone in the group. The most valuable thing you can do is to get people to share their thoughts. That's how the relationships in your group will grow and thrive. Here's a rule: The impact of your study material will typically never exceed the impact of the relationships through which it was studied. The more meaningful the relationships, the more meaningful the study. In a sterile environment, even the best material is suppressed.

3. **Point to the material**—A good host or hostess gets the party going by offering delectable hors d'oeuvres and beverages. You too should be ready to serve up "delicacies" from the material. Sometimes you will simply read the discussion questions and invite

everyone to respond. At other times, you may encourage someone to share his own ideas. Remember, some of the best treats are the ones your guests will bring to the party. Go with the flow of the meeting, and be ready to pop out of the kitchen as needed.

4. **Depart from the material**—A talented ministry team has carefully designed this study for your small group. But that doesn't mean you should follow every part word for word. Knowing how and when to depart from the material is a valuable art. Nobody knows more about your people than you do. The narratives, questions, and exercises are here to provide a framework for discovery. However, every group is motivated differently. Sometimes the best way to start a small-group discussion is simply to ask, "Does anyone have a personal insight or revelation you would like to share from this week's material?" Then sit back and listen.

5. **Stay on track**—Conversation is like the currency of a small-group discussion. The more interchange, the healthier the

"economy." However, you need to keep your objectives in mind. If your goal is to have a meaningful experience with this material, then you should make sure the discussion is contributing to that end. It's easy to get off on a tangent. Be prepared to interject politely and refocus the group. You may need to say something like, "Excuse me, we're obviously all interested in this subject; however, I just want to make sure we cover all the material for this week."

6. **Above all, pray**—The best communicators are the ones who manage to get out of God's way enough to let Him communicate *through* them. That's important to keep in mind. Books don't teach God's Word; neither do sermons or group discussions. God Himself speaks into the hearts of men and women, and prayer is our vital channel to communicate directly with Him. Cover your efforts in prayer. You don't just want God present at your meeting, you want Him to direct it.

We hope you find these suggestions helpful. And we hope you enjoy leading this study. You will find additional guides and suggestions for each session in the Leader's Guide notes that follow.

Leader's Guide Notes

SESSION 1—WE WERE ALL FISH ONCE

KEY POINT

The foundation of our call to be "fishers of men" is the perspective that we too were once in a position of needing to hear the good news about Jesus. Recalling our own need helps us to grasp the importance of answering God's call to "go fish."

EXERCISE—PRAY *WHAT*?!

This first exercise of the series is your first experience together as a group. Don't take it too seriously. Establish the precedent now that this study can be a fun experience. Some people may feel intimidated or overwhelmed at the thought of studying the Bible in a small group. You can help ease their anxieties by not going too deep too soon. The point of this exercise is to initiate conversation about how self-centered our prayer lives tend to be. This is nothing to be ashamed of; but it's worth comparing to God's agenda for our lives.

VIDEO NOTES

1. Most people become Christians for purely <u>selfish</u> motives.
2. The first disciples followed Jesus because of what He did for <u>them</u>.
3. God wants to lead us to become fishers of <u>men</u>.

NOTES FOR DISCUSSION QUESTIONS

1. What are the agendas of most people who become Christians?

   As pointed out in the video message, most people become Christians because of what's in it for them. This question is designed to invite the people in your group to begin interacting with the series. The leader may need to help cultivate open discussion here. Try to encourage everyone to share their opinions.

2. Why do you think the disciples first wanted to follow Jesus?

Obviously, this requires speculation. The purpose of this question is to give partici- pants a chance to respond to what was suggested about Jesus' first followers in the video message. This question will also help to establish that your group is a place where personal opinions are welcome.

3. According to Jesus, what is His agenda for His followers?

Also pointed out in the video message, Jesus promised to make us "fishers of men." Additionally, you may ask for people's

reaction to this discovery. Is it something
they pursue regularly? Is it a new idea?

4. What obstacles keep you from being a fisher
of men?

This question turns the discussion to a more
personal application. Encourage honesty
here. Some people don't fish for men
because they're afraid, selfish, or disinter-
ested. That's okay. The main idea behind
this question is to generate an honest
assessment of where we are with the idea of
fishing for men.

5. Talk about the person who was key in you
becoming a Christian.

This question should help participants put a
face on the fishing process. As they share
about this person, it will also give them an
opportunity to talk about their past experiences and enable group members to get to
know one another better. It should also pre-

pare them for the next question, as they think about the unique role this person had in their lives.

6. Who is someone that God has perfectly positioned you to influence?

Encourage participants to think about their spheres of influence. Everybody has been positioned by God to speak into someone else's life. As participants think about their work environments, their families, their neighbors, and their friends, someone should come to mind.

WHAT WILL YOU DO?

This exercise is intended to bring participants face-to-face with a sense of gratitude that someone once took the time to share Jesus with them. This perspective is an important motivator for answering the call to go fish.

Think About It

This question is designed to help participants begin to analyze how the fishing process works. As they look back on their own experiences as fish, they can begin to see what compelled them to follow Christ. The goal is to become a producer of the same environment that once served them.

SESSION 2—WHY FISH?

KEY POINT

In our culture, there are so many reasons not to fish that it's important to recall why we need to fish. This session explains that Christianity is based on historical events that must be reported in order to be realized; moreover, Christianity is too counterintuitive to be recognized without help. Unless believers tell others about Jesus, they'll never know.

EXERCISE—TURNING POINTS

The purpose of this exercise is to help participants begin to view Jesus' life as a world-changing event in history. Christianity is not simply a belief system, but a response to actual events in history.

VIDEO NOTES

1. Christians believe something <u>happened</u> in history.
2. We think talking about Jesus gets us into a <u>debate</u> about belief systems.
3. Being a fisher of men isn't about having so much <u>knowledge</u> that you can refute the skeptics.

NOTES FOR DISCUSSION QUESTIONS

1. Have you ever seen something so exciting that you couldn't stop talking about it? Describe.

   This question is intended to help partici-pants appreciate what it must have felt like to have physically seen Jesus and to have been excited to talk about Him. The implica-tion is that we should be equally excited about His impact on our lives and desire to share that news with the people around us.

2. What's the difference between sharing something you believe and sharing something you've seen and heard?

This question highlights the big distinction between pushing one's religion and sharing one's faith. We are not called to convince the world of a theology, but simply to share our personal experiences with Jesus. That not only makes our testimonies more authentic, it also relieves a lot of pressure from the fishing process. Furthermore, it forces us to examine just how much we've "seen" Jesus work in our lives.

3. Does being a fisher of men mean convincing someone of your beliefs? Why or why not?

This question simply brings home the concept laid out above. When participants realize that they don't have to convince anyone of anything, they will be more motivated to fish.

4. Have you ever been asked a tough question
   about your faith? How did you respond?

   Encourage participants to think back to their
   spiritual conversations with non-believers.
   Likely, some have not been asked tough
   questions, which illustrates that we don't
   need to fear this possibility in our interac-
   tions with those outside the faith. Likely,
   some have been asked tough questions and
   it is helpful to learn from them how they
   responded.

5. How would your life be different if you had
   never heard anything about Jesus?

   This question puts things in practical terms.
   The implication is that if we don't tell others
   about Jesus, then their lives will be nega-
   tively impacted as well.

WHAT WILL YOU DO?

The purpose of this assignment is to spend more time contemplating some of the differences Christ has made in our
lives. This produces a two-fold benefit. First, it fosters a
deeper sense of gratitude. Second, it helps us recall specific
evidence that we can share with non-believers when we tell
them about Jesus.

THINK ABOUT IT

This assignment will help participants make the connec-
tion between what the first disciples shared and what we
share about Jesus today. Like them, we should simply share
what we've seen and heard. When we recall the dramatic
difference Christ makes in our lives today, it is only natural that we should share that with the people around us.

SESSION 3—FISH GUTS

KEY POINT

Christians in the first century were motivated by the sudden realization that they were living in the midst of God's unfolding plan for the world. As we explore this reality in our lives today, we are equally motivated to go fish.

EXERCISE—THE DADDY DIFFERENCE

This should be a fun exercise. The main point is to establish the concept that we gain courage when we realize that a trustworthy authority is in charge, especially when that authority is pursuing an agenda behind the scenes.

VIDEO NOTES

1. In light of God's sovereignty over the events in their lives, the believers in Acts 4 prayed for <u>boldness</u>.

2. Boldness is simply <u>speaking</u> up when the opportunity pops up.

NOTES FOR DISCUSSION QUESTIONS

1. Why do you think the disciples in Acts 4:31 were filled with boldness?

    By examining the motivation behind the disciples' courage, we can begin to find similar motivation in our own lives. God is just as large and in charge today as He was in the first century.

2. How would your life be different if you truly believed God was in control?

    This question is designed to foster more vision casting. Most of our limits in life are self-imposed. This question will help partici-pants think about just how bold they can be in life, knowing that God is fully in control of everything. We don't have to fear men. That doesn't mean we should be irresponsible, tactless, or impatient in our fishing styles. But we don't have to be timid either.

3. What are the threats that deter you from speaking God's Word boldly?

It can be very helpful to identify the obstacles that hold us back from sharing the message of Jesus with boldness. Once we recognize the source of our fears and hindrances, we can begin to resolve them. A problem well-defined is a problem half-solved.

4. How might God use those threats for His own glory?

Furthermore, as this question implies, the things we perceive as obstacles are often opportunities for God to show up in our midst. This question hearkens back to the situation in Acts 4, reminding us that what we consider losses or setbacks are negligible to God.

5. How do your prayers differ from the one prayed in Acts 4?

This question should trigger some personal introspection as participants examine how closely their prayers resemble those modeled in Scripture. Encourage honesty here. Are there any changes that need to be made in the way we pray?

6. Have you ever asked God to enable you to speak with boldness? Why or why not?

As this question suggests, participants might consider making boldness an objective for their spiritual growth—beginning with asking God for it.

7. What would "bold" look like in your life?

This is another vision-casting question. Encourage the group to share ideas of practical ways to be bold about their faith. You might begin with ideas that are simple and achievable for anyone.

What Will You Do?

Participants will likely be surprised at the difference they notice when they begin to pray daily for boldness. First, they will be more attuned to the opportunities that arise. Second, they will gain steady confidence as God increases boldness within them.

Think About It

Similar to the last question of the study, this application step will get the participants to think of a practical next step they can take in the life of a non-Christian. It is important to distinguish here between "bold" and obnoxious. They don't need to be over-the-top in their next interaction. Rather, they need to take a simple next step.

SESSION 4—FISHING BUDDIES

KEY POINT

Fishing was never meant to be a solo endeavor. Whenever two or more are gathered in Jesus' name, God is there in their midst. Our fishing is more effective when we partner with other believers—whether one or two individuals, or a local church group. Seeing the body of Christ in action is the closest a person can get in this life to being in the presence of Jesus Himself.

EXERCISE—COME AND SEE

The purpose of this exercise is to demonstrate the power of witnessing something first-hand, versus hearing it explained as a principle or a belief system. When we see the body of Christ in action, it says much more about Jesus than a person could learn by examining Christian beliefs.

VIDEO NOTES

1. Being in a community of believers breaks down the barriers to <u>unbelief</u>.

2. When the church is organized and strategized around official <u>Jesus</u> business, Jesus shows up in their midst.

3. The <u>church</u> is the most powerful, persuasive environment on the planet.

NOTES FOR DISCUSSION QUESTIONS

1. Do you tend to think of evangelism as a solo expedition or a partnership? Why?

   This is an introductory question designed to expose current perceptions of the fishing process.

2. What are some of the biggest differences
   between evangelizing alone and partnering
   with other believers to fish for men?

   This question should unearth some basic
   points that were presented in the video message—as with almost any undertaking, two
   are better than one.

3. Would you be comfortable inviting a non-
   believer to your church? Why or why not?

   This question will prompt participants to
   take an honest look at their current church
   situation. What works? What doesn't? If
   there are any deficiencies in terms of the
   church acting as a partner in the fishing
   process, this question will expose them.

4. Describe an environment in which you would be comfortable inviting a non-believing friend to hear more about Jesus.

   This question is designed to trigger some vision-casting. It encourages participants to start from scratch and envision the ideal environment for fishing. When we eliminate all preconceptions about church, it's easier to assess the true value of various church activities.

5. How would you follow up with a friend after he attended church (or another environment) with you?

   This question builds on the previous question causing them to think through their invitations to friends. Often a simple conversation about what the person thought is a great follow-up.

6. Is there an event in the next month to which you could invite a friend? How would you extend this invitation?

   Building further from the previous two questions, this question puts an action plan in place that will lead participants to apply the key points of this session.

What Will You Do?

This exercise looks backwards at what our idea of "fishing for men" looked like before this session. This will highlight the contrast between where we are and where we could be. In light of what has been learned in this session, it should lead the participant to conclude that some changes need to take place.

Think About It

Revisiting the questions in the discussion section, this assignment allows the participants to distill their initial thoughts into concrete action plans.

SESSION 5—MUDDY WATER

KEY POINT

Unless we are able to articulate the message of Jesus clearly and effectively, our efforts to be fishers of men will be hindered. Surprisingly, few Christians are skilled at making a simple presentation of the gospel. Often, we overcomplicate it. This is a very practical session designed to teach participants a simple presentation of the gospel that can be shared with others.

EXERCISE—KEEP IT SIMPLE

This familiar childhood game helps to demonstrate our natural tendency to confuse a simple message.

VIDEO NOTES

1. To become a Christian, a person needs to know that:

   God <u>loved</u>.

   God <u>gave</u> His son.

2. To become a Christian:

We need to <u>believe</u> in the work of Jesus.

Then, we <u>have</u> the gift of eternal life.

Notes for Discussion Questions

1. Why do you think Christians make Christianity so complicated?

   This is an introductory question that simply provides a venue for participants to reach the overwhelming conclusion that Christians tend to complicate the gospel.

2. How do you think the average person would describe the requirements for getting into heaven?

   Digging deeper, this question will prompt participants to look at some of the common ways we complicate the message of Christ.

3. How would you describe those requirements in light of this session?

This is a very important exercise that allows everyone in your group to personalize the content of this session. If they can answer this question, they can present the gospel.

4. Name two people in your sphere of influence who don't know that God loves them and forgives them.

This question is designed to help participants begin to visualize actually sharing a simple gospel presentation with someone around them.

5. If you had to guess, what are some of the complications that have prevented them from understanding God's simple message?

In very real terms, this question will reveal the drawbacks of complicating the gospel;

in addition, it will suggest the value of pre-
senting the gospel in simple terms to these
people.

What Will You Do?

This is an obvious but very important assignment. It's
purpose is to ensure that each participant can give a
simple gospel presentation whenever an opportunity
presents itself.

Think About It

This exercise ties the simple gospel message together with
the concept of sharing what we've "seen and heard." The
idea is to be able to share the message of John 3:16 from a
personal perspective (i.e. "What Jesus did for me was….").

SESSION 6—THE ONE THAT GOT AWAY

KEY POINT

As a final perspective, this session leaves participants with the perspective that failing to take the initiative to share Jesus with others is tantamount to hoarding a great blessing for themselves.

EXERCISE—I FORGOT

Being forgetful is often a simple matter of becoming self-absorbed. This exercise is designed to suggest that being proactive about sharing Jesus requires a conscious decision to take initiative in this area.

VIDEO NOTES

1. The lepers said to each other, "We're not doing <u>right</u>."

2. If we're not careful, our tendency will be to forget to go <u>back</u>.

NOTES FOR DISCUSSION QUESTIONS

1. Why do Christians often forget to "go back" and share the good news with others who need it?

   This question reveals some obvious but valuable truths about our nature as Christians. In any case, most of us simply need to recognize our responsibility to share Jesus with others.

2. What riches do you enjoy that need to be shared with others?

   This question provides a tangible tie-in with the Bible story from the video message. Like the lepers, our first tendency is to hoard our blessings.

3. What would it look like in your life to "cross the desert" just to tell them?

   This question revisits some of the vision-casting questions of earlier sessions in which participants envision scenarios where they share Christ; however, this time it is in the context of the story of the lepers.

4. How might it change their lives to discover God's riches?

   Similarly, this question helps participants to envision the spiritual hunger that exists until we provide the good news of Jesus to those who desperately need it.

5. From the perspective of those watching from heaven, what do you think is the "obvious" thing for you to do?

   As was suggested in the video message, when we hear the story of the lepers, it's obvious what they should do. This question invites participants to take a similar, objective look at their lives. They will likely conclude that sharing Christ is the only logical response.

WHAT WILL YOU DO?

On a very practical level, this assignment is designed to encourage everyone to become intentional about sharing the message of Jesus. Identifying specific people will sharpen our focus and make us more aware of opportunities.

THINK ABOUT IT

Building on the previous exercise, this assignment encourages them to be proactive. Rather than waiting for opportunities to materialize, this step suggests that we can work alongside God to help initiate those opportunities.

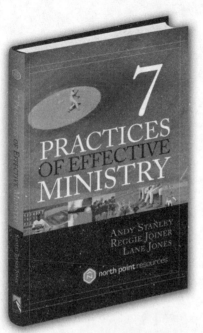

7 Practices of Effective Ministry

by Andy Stanley, Reggie Joiner, and Lane Jones

ISBN 1-59052-373-3

Rethink Your Ministry Game Plan

Succeeding in sports means victory, winning! But what does it mean in your ministry? An insightful and entertaining parable for every church leader who yearns for a more simplified approach to ministry.

Creating Community

by Andy Stanley and Bill Willits

ISBN 1-59052-396-2

Form Small Groups That Succeed

To build a healthy, thriving small-group environment you need a plan. Here are five proven principles from one of the most successful small-group ministry churches in the country. Learn them, implement them, and empower God's people to truly do life together.

north point resources

Parental Guidance Required
by Andy Stanley and Reggie Joiner
DVD: ISBN 1-59052-378-4
Study Guide: ISBN 1-59052-381-4

Influence Your Child's Future
Our lives are shaped by relationships, experiences, and decisions. Therefore, our priority as parents should be to enhance our child's relationship with us, advance our child's relationship with God, and influence our child's relationship with those outside the home.

Discovering God's Will
by Andy Stanley
DVD: ISBN 1-59052-380-6
Study Guide: ISBN 1-59052-379-2

Make Decisions with Confidence
God has a personal vision for your life and He wants you to know it even more than you do. Determining God's will can be a difficult process, especially when we need to make a decision in a hurry. In this series Andy Stanley leads us through God's providential, moral, and personal will.

The Best Question Ever
by Andy Stanley
DVD: ISBN 1-59052-463-2
Study Guide: ISBN 1-59052-462-4

Foolproof Your Life
When it comes to sorting out the complexities of each unique situation we face, only wisdom can reveal the best path. The question posed here will empower you to make regretless decisions every time.

north point resources

Defining Moments
by Andy Stanley
DVD: ISBN 1-59052-465-9
Study Guide: ISBN 1-59052-464-0

Because Ignorance Is Not Bliss...
What you don't know CAN hurt you. But we still go out of our way at times to avoid the truth. In *Defining Moments*, we discover individuals of the Bible who embraced the truth as Jesus made it clear to them, and how the truth set them free indeed.

Taking Care of Business
by Andy Stanley
DVD: ISBN 1-59052-492-6
Study Guide: ISBN 1-59052-491-8

Finding God at Work
God created work and intends for us to make the most of it! Gain His perspective and get equipped to make changes that allow you to thrive in the workplace.

Life Rules
by Andy Stanley
DVD: ISBN 1-59052-494-2
Study Guide: ISBN 1-59052-493-4

Instructions for Life
God's guidelines for living are for your protection and freedom. Learn them, live by them, and experience the dramatic, positive change in every area of your life.

north point resources